Redemption

Redemption

A Poetic Journey

Sean Ewing

RESOURCE *Publications* · Eugene, Oregon

REDEMPTION
A Poetic Journey

Resource Publications
An Imprint of Wipf and Stock Publishers
199 W. 8th Ave., Suite 3
Eugene, OR 97401

www.wipfandstock.com

PAPERBACK ISBN: 978-1-6667-1676-4
HARDCOVER ISBN: 978-1-6667-1677-1
EBOOK ISBN: 978-1-6667-1678-8

JULY 1, 2021

All poetry and images created by Sean Ewing

To Catherine my excellent wife, lover, and best friend.
Thank you for all that you have taught me, for exemplifying
faithfulness, forgiveness, and compassion as we journey
through this life of faith.

Contents

Part Three

~ REDEEMED ~

Preface

THE GOSPEL IS THE redemption plan God has taken, purely at His initiative and in keeping with His own purposes, to reconcile the relationship between Himself and wayward mankind. That relationship was eternally broken when the first man and woman disobeyed His commandment to them, a directive given in love intending to deepen their relationship with God. For reconciliation to occur, two seemingly contradictory qualities of God's nature had to be satisfied: His justice and His love.

God's justice required that mankind's rebellion had to be judged and punished. As the Bible says, "For the wages of sin is death, but the gift of God is eternal life in Christ Jesus our Lord." (Romans 3:23) At the same time, God's love moved Him to extend mercy, forgiveness, to His wayward creation. His love sought a redemption plan to provide restoration to a lost mankind.

God's loving plan of redemption is through the act of Jesus Christ, God's Son, coming into this world and becoming a willing atoning sacrifice, personally taking the full weight of God's judgment against mankind's sin rebellion. Having lived a sinless life completely in accord with God's will, Jesus was able to offer His life as a perfect substitution. God's Son, conceived by the Holy Spirit and born of a woman, He was unique – fully human, yet fully God. Jesus offered Himself, the only sufficient sacrifice to bear God's judgment on the world.

Jesus' atoning work required His suffering and death. Though sinless and innocent of any crime, He was falsely accused by religious leaders, rejected by the crowd that had praised him just days before, and condemned by the Roman governor. Executed by crucifixion, Jesus died and was buried in a tomb. On the third day following His death, He was resurrected, fully alive, showing Himself to the disciples who had followed Him. This story of Christ, of the deliverance and restoration of mankind's sin problem, the redemption, we have victory in Christ through His life, sacrificial death, and resurrection. This is rooted in the historical witness of those first followers and countless numbers who've since believed their testimony and experienced the reality of God's loving salvation by grace through faith.

We must each recognize ourselves to be sinners, separated from God and alienated by our own disobedience. As descendants of the original rebels, we are, by nature, disposed toward resisting God and His will. Only with God's help, are we able to see our wrong for what it is and experience the fear and regret that such conviction brings.

The first step toward salvation is seeing the need for it and, that we are lost, God must help us. Only God can change a human heart. Only then are we open to God's mercy and kindness. Seeing our deep need, we hear the declaration of God's mercy, of Christ taking our punishment and making a way for us to find peace with God. The prospect of deliverance from the judgment of sin and restored relationship with the Father is achieved purely on the basis of God's work in Christ, without reliance upon any work of our own.

It is in the simple act of faith, of confessing who Jesus is as Savior and believing that God raised him from the dead that we receive the gift of salvation. The mercy He offers and the new life He gives are embraced through the exercise of faith as we yield our lives to Him who has done so much for us.

This book of poetry is a journey of thoughts, emotions, and convictions on the road to redemption. As a writer of poetry, I am influenced by Sylvia Plath and Anne Sexton who brought to us a brand of confessional poetry that has always been impactful in my life. I believe as a follower of Christ to be confessional is biblical and necessary (First John 1:9-10). I believe it is necessary to understand the impacts of my sin and the choices I make. This poetical journey will bring the reader into this working process to understand life and sin and eventually salvation and redemption in Christ. In all that follows is an underpinning of what the Bible teaches us about salvation. This is an important fact, yes, this poetry is art, but my attempt is to be biblically and theologically sound that can perhaps in new ways teach us about the process of salvation (ordo salutis). It speaks of a way of organizing all the events of redemption in the order that they show up in an individual's life when the repentant sinner, saved by grace through faith (Ephesians 2:8) is joined to Christ.

April 2021
Sean Ewing

Part One

～ Lost ～

Followed

We met as kids and became friends soon thereafter
Childhood friendship with lots of laughter
It wasn't long until his hands grasped a dagger
I can say I was surprised to see the steely tool
I tried to think it wasn't true, but I'm a fool
The poniard was planted with skill and a smile
Landing on target just left of center into my back
The gripping memory of disappointment
The pain of betrayal and loss
The knife wasn't just in my back
The wound was deeper than that
It went through my back and broke my heart
I have been bleeding out ever since
The unquietness of bitterness
I'm being followed by an unforgiven past

November

My sorrow is ever present
An ever-spiraling descent
My hopes in life are gone and fled
I'm left with this dark feeling of dread
My life is a gloomy November day
Desolate trees reaching out to gray cloudy skies
Like bony fingers grasping disappointment
I want to forgive but I don't
Like a cold merciless wind
That stings my face I regret instead
Regret spawns no fruit
No flowers
No warmth
November, the time of the dead and dying

Black Rose

I am hatred, it's something I bleed
I cry at night, longing to be freed
The rain, the flood, the grief
I am morose, a dismal, ravaged life
My life, my past is pain
What remains is disdain
My tears are my truest friends
This, my heart, a dying sun
A flower faded to black
A pallid sun sheds dimmest glow
And I feel as though I won't escape
The cold grip of pain and regret
In this numbing empty space called my heart

Drowning

The face of nemesis
The pressure of expectations
My yearning whisper of desperation
In this world of deceit
To lie, to cry, and sigh
I'm drowning in a life of lies
I'm drowning where hope dies
The pain I cause bears my name
Ignorance dies by its own lies
Crying under a sunless sky
My tears of bitterness
To lie, to cry, and sigh
I'm drowning in a life of lies
I'm drowning where hope dies
My life is like a tattered flag
Beaten in the cold north wind
That relentless cold that kills
Of frost and war, oppressed dominion
To lie, to cry, and sigh
I'm drowning in a life of lies
I'm drowning where hope dies

Leaves

Am I connected?
To something much larger
Then just myself and my misery?
A single connected leaf
In a canopy of verdant life
For a season, for a moment
Connected to life and love
Once draped in lively beauty
Now a change to remorseful russet
Summer fades like tears in vain
The grief of life and heart
Changing, becoming a faded memory
Autumn's cold and icy wind
Dying leaves fringed with ice crystals
Sparkling in the morning sun
A glimmering announcement
That the end is near
The autumn winds
Stress the dying connection
Separated into the driven wind
A life that was, is drifting now
Down to where the wind directs
Drifting north, northwest
South, northwest, west
Landing among the mass of dead leaves
I am a languishing leaf in descent
Once connected but no more
Where am I going?
Anywhere the wind blows

Winter

Contractive force that drains color and life
Winter sun setting over monochrome landscape
Like an angel flying too close to the ground
Creating a world of subtle amber glow
Softened by chilled gray mist and fog
Icicles hang from the edge of my heart
Barely alive as love departs
In frozen stillness of a long winter night
Grief has worn my heart into stone
As quiet as a cat on cotton
Winter has gripped my heart
Alone I stare into the frost's white face
For those I loved I hurt
Ice cold pain of unforgiveness

Running

I have got to get out of here
Running away from problems, lies and fear
Running from God and life
Running away from truth
A sip of the whisky of life
A sip of the wine of life
Feel it in the morning
This whisky this wine
This so-called life
I'm still willing
Run to oblivion with contempt at my side
To run from failure and pain
To run from grief and disappointment
Greasy easy whisky wine
Partake of this doomsday communion

Conceal

Hiding from retribution
Hiding my face
My shame and my disgrace
Burying sorrow and pain
Drained of peace, what remains is disdain
So much to say yet unspoken
The heart of pain and suffering
As I conceal how I feel
Love has no face
As darkness fills that space
False is the face that hides the pain
I wear a mask to conceal how I feel
Behind my concealing mask I am less afraid
Something disingenuous is portrayed
The mask is not who any of us are
It's to conceal a heart and its ugly scar

Loneliness

Lonely is the long dark night
Where peace is nowhere in sight
A lonely tear runs down
As the moonlight reveals my frown
Those lonely tears escape
My lifetime of mistakes
On a lonely night like this
As a cloud obscures the moonlight
Peering through the fog and mist
I long to see the hope of light
In the darkness of my loneliness
I long for the warmth of light
To end this dark lonely night
Lonely are footsteps of a departing friend
Lonely is solitude of nights that will not end
Lonely are my tears on a cold cheek
Lonely is silence of sorrows too deep to speak
As I look upon the dark lonely sky
It doesn't matter how hard I try
Wanting a lifetime of painful memories to die
I just can't hide these lonely eyes

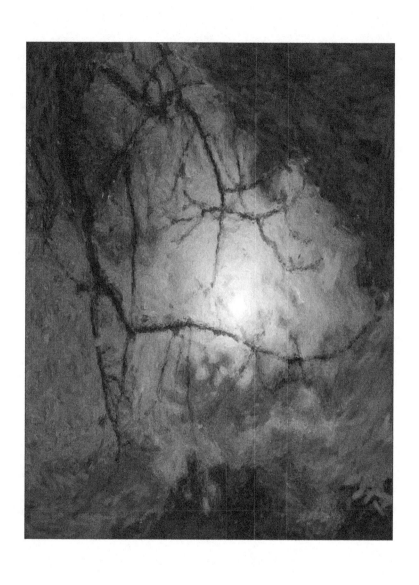

Waves

I feel the depth of the ocean's darkness
As the cold furious waves pound the shore
Creating a cold spray that stings my face
Waves of pain and sorrow
Waves the color of wet cement
Bring the weight of despair and hopelessness
Each wave is a problem in my life
Waves crashing along the shore
They take out of me a little more
From deep darkness underneath the sea
The waves keep crashing into me
These waves from the mighty ocean swell
Assail upon my craggy rock of a life
Their raging fury shakes me to the core
A cold stinging salty spray, please no more
Doomed to imprisonment which knows no end
Living in gloomy depths of tribulation

Part Two

~ Seeking ~

Glow

Frosty winter night shivering in the snow
Is there hope to make my heart glow?
To melt a frozen heart in the depths of despair
God, I cry out to you in my desperate prayer
God's mercy and grace blow the coals into flame
To end my misery and life of shame
Love is the flame, grace is the glow
Warming my heart
For a new start
Drifting away the pain of life
Lifting away all the strife

Glimmer of Hope

Perhaps I am mistaken
But I feel forsaken
When life gets difficult
A confusing tumult
Where are my friends?
Has it come to this end?
This forsaken emptiness?
Perhaps I am mistaken
But am I alone?
Chilled to the bone
By the cold shoulder of life
I'm yearning for a smiling tomorrow
Void of pain, grief, and sorrow
Hurt runs deep in my heart
Some days it wants to fall apart
But I have a glimmer of hope
I am longer at the end of my rope
My whispering desperate prayer
Merciful God is all I need, ending my despair

Problems

I wish my problems would just die
Oh, to be sent away and let fly
Are my problems endless?
Thinking so just leaves me breathless
I often wonder how I keep going
Knowing full well my anguish is showing
I want to say end all this
Please be dismissed
Problems, you won't be missed
What else can I do to cope?
Where oh God is hope?
Can my hope be in you?
My heart yearns for Your love
Hope in Your compassion and care
To survive another day
To conquer the problems of my life of sin

Window

Looking out the window of my life
I stand here wondering what could have been
Swelling tears in diaries of lies
That place where expectation dies
Dissatisfaction fills most human hearts
Discontented, we stay mostly in life
Looking out through the window
Desiring and looking for love
Oh God I need your love from above
A voice to speak to me in comfort
A hand to touch me in this dark room
Breaking through the long loneliness
God, I look to You and Your holiness

Rain

Never really could explain
How I always loved the rain
Never really could explain
How I caused so much pain
Beginning now to understand
Rain must fall
And it does
Over and over
My tears rain down
Upon my past
Can I get past my past?
Blue skies are clear in the future
Even as rain, she keeps falling now
I should have no fear as I look to God
God, I cry out to You now

Shipwreck

Oh life! So messy
Travelling along the restless seas
The turmoil and chaos of rough waters
As I am tossed blindly on this midnight sea
Rising and falling with the waves
Friends and family are drifting away from me
Like lifeboats from a shipwreck
Broken pieces of relationships and cold emotions
Are sinking in deep salty sea
Like a ship gnashing of metal, I groan
God, I feel your voice tugging at my heart
At night when I hear you calling across the waters
I want to land this shipwrecked life
Upon the shores of your unfailing love

Shoulder to Cry

By habit, I complain when things go wrong
Discontentment has been my life
But I'm tired of being discontent
I look to God to help me
I'm curious to understand
To stay away from despair
To recognize the voice of God
Chasing dreams that never come
As a result, I have become undone
True friends are rare
Longing to feel love and grace
The winds of change are needed
Here I am once again
Suppressing my feelings and pain
I need a shoulder to cry on
God, I desire freedom from regretting the past
Even though the love in my life didn't last
My life doesn't have to end this way
God, forgive me help me conquer feelings of dismay

Change

A change in perspective
will change a field of weeds
Into a meadow of flowers
A change in perspective
will change a barren wasteland
into a field of opportunity
A change in perspective
will change a bleak dismal life
into a life of peace and sweet rest
I want change in my life
I seek, pray, and ask gracious God
For a change in my heart
To change the way my story ends
To change goals and sights I see
God only you can change my heart
My direction, my reflection
A chance for love and new beginnings
Leaving the old way of thinking and its shortcomings
Life is a long journey
Full of uncertainties, ups and downs
Alas! A beautiful journey can begin
In faith with God as the light upon my path

Part Three

∼ Redeemed ∼

Surrender

To you Lord Jesus, I surrender my heart
I surrender all my faults and sins to You
I surrender now to You Lord, new life new start
All to You my Lord and Savior I give
In Your loving embrace I now live
Salvation in Christ sweet satisfaction
Crying out to You with outstretched arms
Desire now to serve You in thought and action
Only You do I desire to please
I humbly surrender to You in prayer
Lord, give me faith to know You are there

Salvation

God provided a way of salvation
For all the people of his creation
God sent Jesus to die upon the cross
Because of Jesus we don't suffer such a loss
Christ's gift of salvation freely given
All so we could be forgiven
Jesus died upon the cross for our sin
God's love, Christ's death allows us heaven above
Jesus' death and resurrection, everlasting love
Jesus loves, he suffered and bled for me and you
He is the only one that would go to the cross for me and you
It was for all sinners like me and you that Jesus died
Confess and trust Jesus as Savior and forever with him abide
My whole life I have been in rebellion and sin
I confess my sin to my Savior Jesus, new life can begin
My whole life I have been a harvester of sorrow
Your forgiveness, grace, and mercy a new tomorrow

Free

No longer a sheep gone astray
Jesus my Savior provided the way
I can live and be free of sin and death
He saved me on the cross in His dying breath
I never could imagine so great a light
Could conquer the sin of my darkest night
In Christ I am free from sin
The Lord saved me, the end of my chagrin
From bondage of sin, I am free
Praising the Lord on bended knee

Song

Today I can sing a new song
Because to Christ I now belong
I will never sing those songs I had all along
Songs of sadness and melancholy
New songs of hope
Songs of love
Songs of adoration
For the God of love and hope
For the God of salvation, grace and mercy
Songs of true love and songs of true freedom

Watercolor

I walked into the ocean of Your forgiveness
Forgiveness of my sins because of Jesus
In Your ocean of forgiveness
Sins are like watercolors
My sins wash out
Washed out in a tide of enduring love
The sacrifice of my savior, my Jesus
What was a life of crimson sin
Is now a life forgiven and white as snow
A new canvas can begin with the master's touch
New colors of life enlightened in Christ
God, may my life be a canvas for Your expression

Soar

Freer than most birds an eagle flies up into the sky
Up above where we can hear a conquering cry
He climbs and glides over land and water
My, how majestic is the eagle's soar
Free to roam, the skies as conqueror
Like the eagle who conquers the skies
I too in Christ can conquer all the lies
Lies to bring me down no more
In Christ I am an eagle meant to soar

New Life

Warm summer breezes blow
Prairie flowers wave a greeting below
White fluffy clouds float on high
Against the bright blue sky
I have found the light to end my long dark night
Brighter than any stars or sun oh what a sight
I have lost any fear of the past so dreary
All the worries and pain that made me weary
The raging storms have passed by
I can now stand and not wonder why
Standing while my loving God holds my hand
I feel a thrill that I never used to feel
New life in Christ, nothing now to conceal
So, let it be, as I cling to my great God
There is nothing in my life to dread
Because Jesus conquered sin when he bled
In Christ I am a new life instead
Unlike the days when my heart was dead

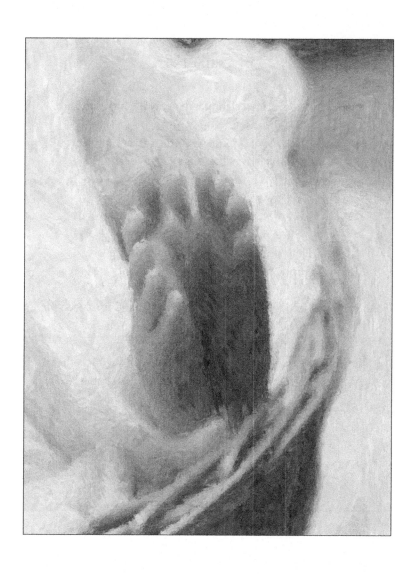

My Psalm 145

God is here I want to celebrate; may my life be perpetual
celebration of You
Announce to the world God's presence, grace, and mercy
How compassionate He is over all creation
How tender He is toward us his failure fraught people
Yet always faithful to His promises
He is just and forgiving
He gently picks me up when I fall
He restores me to sonship and service
In my wavering faith and weakness, He grants me grace
and strength
God reached into the empty void of my heart and produced life
A heart hungry to honor and obey You
He hears my every cry for mercy and grace
How incomparably glorious are You my great loving Father
May my life demonstrate Your loving kindness and grace
Proclaim Your eternal mercy and goodness

Made in the USA
Monee, IL
17 November 2023

46818617R00044